Machines Then and Now

Robert Quinn

Contents

OXFORD
UNIVERSITY PRESS

OXFORD
UNIVERSITY PRESS

Great Clarendon Street, Oxford OX2 6DP

Oxford University Press is a department of the University of Oxford. It furthers the University's objective of excellence in research, scholarship, and education by publishing worldwide in

Oxford New York

Auckland Cape Town Dar es Salaam Hong Kong Karachi
Kuala Lumpur Madrid Melbourne Mexico City Nairobi
New Delhi Shanghai Taipei Toronto

With offices in

Argentina Austria Brazil Chile Czech Republic France
Greece Guatemala Hungary Italy Japan Poland Portugal
Singapore South Korea Switzerland Thailand Turkey
Ukraine Vietnam

OXFORD and OXFORD ENGLISH are registered trade marks of Oxford University Press in the UK and in certain other countries

© Oxford University Press 2010

The moral rights of the author have been asserted

Database right Oxford University Press (maker)

First published 2010
2014 2013 2012 2011
10 9 8 7 6 5

ISBN: 978 0 19 464437 2

An Audio CD Pack containing this book and a CD is also available
ISBN: 978 0 19 464477 8
The CD has a choice of American and British English recordings of the complete text.

An accompanying Activity Book is also available
ISBN: 978 0 19 464447 1

Printed in China

This book is printed on paper from certified and well-managed sources.

ACKNOWLEDGEMENTS

Illustrations by: Mark Duffin pp3 (computer), 6, 7, 21, 34, 40; Roger at KJA Artists pp3, 4, 5, 8, 9, 24; Alan Rowe pp24, 26, 28, 30, 32, 36, 46, 47; Gary Swift p15.

The publisher would like to thank the following for their kind permission to reproduce photographs and other copyright material: Alamy Images pp3 (Alarm clock/studiomode), 9 (Container terminal, Germany/ blickwinkel), 13 (Alarm clock/studiomode), 22 (Bucket wheel excavator/F1online digitale Bildagentur GmbH), 42 (Bucket wheel excavator/F1online digitale Bildagentur GmbH); Corbis pp16 (Lincoln Beachey Airship/H. Armstrong Roberts), 20 (Man working with early computer/Jerry Cooke), p23 (Denso micro-car 1995 model/TWPhoto); p42 (Denso micro-car 1995 model/ TWPhoto); Getty Images pp3 (Corporate jet/Paul Bowen), 8 (Giza pyramids/James L. Stanfield), 10 (Glade Creek Grist Mill, USA/Ron and Patty Thomas), 17 (Corporate jet/Paul Bowen), 18 (Portable television 1949); Hemera Technologies Inc. pp18 (Old fashioned telephone), 18 (Old fashioned radio); iStockphoto p11 (Wind turbines in wind farm/Brian Jackson); Mirrorpix p14 (Steam train); OUP pp7 (London Eye/Image Source), 13 (clock detail/Design Pics); PA Photos pp17 (World's Smallest Helicopter/Lorenzo Galassi/AP), 19 (Sony 0.3 millimeter display/ AP); Photolibrary pp3 (Electric cars charging/Shmuel Thaler), 9 (Parthenon, Athens, Greece/Goodshoot), 12 (Sundial/The Irish Image Collection), p13 (Brass gears from a pocket watch/ Corbis); 15 (Electric cars charging/Shmuel Thaler); Robert Harding World Imagery p11 (Thatched windmill/Peter Scholey); Science Photo Library p23 (Nanorobot in the bloodstream/ Christian Darkin).

Introduction

Machines make our lives easier. We use them to do work, to travel, to communicate, and to have fun. Some machines are simple, with only one or two parts. Other machines are complex, with many parts that work together.

What are the machines below called?
What do we do with these machines?
Which of these machines do you use?
What other machines do you use?

Now read and discover more about machines!

The First Machines

People invented the first machines a long time ago. They were simple tools made of stone, wood, or bone.

axe

knife

arrow

bow

lever

About two million years ago people made stone axes with wooden handles. They used these tools to cut wood. People also used stone and animal bone to make knives and arrows. To shoot their arrows they used bows made with long pieces of wood.

People used simple levers to move heavy objects like rocks. They put one end of a long stick of wood under a big rock, and they put a small rock under the stick. When they pushed on the other end of the stick, the big rock moved.

plow

lever

About 7,000 years ago people started farming for food. They invented new machines, like plows, and used animals to make work easier. Some farmers used long levers to get water from rivers. They also built canals to get water for their plants.

About 5,000 years ago people started making metal tools. These tools were better than stone or bone tools.

→ Go to pages 24–25 for activities.

The wheel is one of the most important inventions in history. About 5,500 years ago potters used the first wheels to make clay pots. They put wet clay on a wooden wheel. Then they turned the wheel to make a nice round pot.

Before people had wheels to move heavy objects, they used rollers. The rollers were made from tree trunks. Then people made carts and chariots with wooden wheels. They connected the wheels with a long bar called an axle.

Today there are lots of machines with wheels. We can see wheels on cars, bicycles, and skateboards. There are also wheelchairs for people who can't walk easily. Can you think of more machines that have wheels?

Discover!

The London Eye is a very big wheel. It's 135 meters high! You get a great view of London from the top!

→ Go to pages 26–27 for activities.

Ramps and Cranes

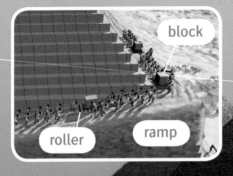

block

roller

ramp

The Pyramids at Giza, Egypt

Ramps are useful because they help us lift objects more easily. More than 5,000 years ago the Ancient Egyptians used ramps to build pyramids. The Great Pyramid at Giza is the biggest pyramid in the world. It's 138 meters high.

The Egyptians used rollers to move large blocks of stone up the ramps. They needed lots of workers because the blocks were very heavy.

pulley

crane

About 2,500 years ago the Ancient Greeks used big cranes to build temples. The cranes were made of wood, and they had many ropes and little wheels called pulleys. First the workers tied a rope to a block of stone. Then they put the rope around the pulley. They pulled the rope and lifted the block. The work was easier with cranes, so the Greeks didn't need as many workers as the Egyptians.

Discover!

We use cranes today to lift very heavy objects. The biggest type of crane is the gantry crane.

→ Go to pages 28–29 for activities.

Some machines use energy from nature. Watermills use energy from flowing water. Thousands of years ago people built watermills next to rivers. They used the watermills to make flour from grain. Then they used the flour to make bread and cakes. Watermills have a big wheel on the outside. The river turns the wheel. Then the wheel turns an axle inside the watermill. The axle turns a round millstone that breaks the grain into flour.

Windmills use energy from the wind. Hundreds of years ago people started using windmills to make flour. Windmills have long arms with big sails. The wind pushes the sails and turns the arms. Inside the mill, an axle turns a millstone. Windmills are useful in places that don't have big rivers, but they only work when it's windy!

sail

arm

Discover!

Today we use windmills to make electricity. Modern windmills are called wind turbines.

Go to pages 30–31 for activities.

pointer

shadow

A Sundial

In the past, people told the time in many ways. Thousands of years ago people used sundials. Sundials had a pointer that made a shadow to tell the time. A sundial only worked on sunny days!

Some people also used water clocks. Simple water clocks had two pots. Water flowed from the top pot to the bottom pot to tell the time. Later, people used sand clocks. These clocks had two glass bubbles with sand inside them.

spring

gears

About 1,000 years ago people invented mechanical clocks with metal gears. Some mechanical clocks have a pendulum to move the parts. Others have metal springs.

Today many clocks are digital. They show the time with only numbers. Digital clocks work with electricity. They usually have electrical cords or batteries. Computers and cell phones have digital clocks, and many people wear digital watches.

→ Go to pages 32–33 for activities.

For thousands of years people used animals to do work. Then inventors built steam engines. These engines heated water to make steam. The energy from the steam made other machines work. The first steam engines usually used fuels like wood, coal, or oil.

People used steam engines to power vehicles like trains and boats. Many factories used steam engines to power their machines. This was the beginning of modern industry.

Then people invented new engines that used fuels like oil, gasoline, and diesel. Now we use these engines for vehicles like cars, buses, planes, or helicopters. They can carry enough fuel to travel long distances.

Today most vehicles use gasoline or diesel as fuel. Some vehicles use biodiesel made from plant materials. There are also electric cars that use energy from batteries. Some vehicles, like bicycles, use human energy!

Discover!

Electric cars are good for the environment. They don't produce smoke or pollution.

→ Go to pages 34–35 for activities.

 7 Flying Machines

Today we can fly all over the world, but 200 years ago planes didn't exist. Some people flew in hot-air balloons. These balloons had no engines so they were slow and hard to control.

An Airship

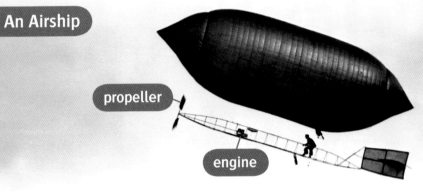

propeller

engine

Later, people invented airships. They had engines and propellers, so they were faster and easier to control.

In 1903 Wilbur and Orville Wright invented the first plane. It was made of wood and carried one person. The first flight only lasted for 12 seconds! Four years later a French inventor named Paul Comu flew one of the first helicopters. He stayed in the air for about 20 seconds.

Today there are many types of plane. Some planes have propellers and others have jet engines. Some planes carry freight and others carry passengers. Some modern planes carry more than 850 passengers!

Helicopters are very useful. They can transport food and medicine in emergencies. They can also rescue people and take them to hospital.

Discover!
The *GEN H-4* is the smallest helicopter in the world. It carries one person!

➔ Go to pages 36–37 for activities.

Communications

For a long time, people sent messages on paper. Then people invented new machines to communicate more quickly and easily.

In 1876 Alexander Graham Bell invented the telephone. It transmitted sounds through wires.

In 1895 Guglielmo Marconi invented the radio. It transmitted sounds with no wires.

In 1926 John Logie Baird invented a way to transmit images and show them on a screen. It was the first television, but it only showed black and white images. Then 18 years later, inventors made a television that showed images in color.

Communications today are very different. We talk on cell phones that transmit sounds with no wires. We can send text messages, photos, and videos. Many cell phones are also music players, and they can connect to the Internet!

With modern televisions, we can receive programs by satellite. We can also watch DVDs. Some televisions are very big. There is a television in Japan that is 11 meters tall and 66 meters long!

Discover!
Some modern televisions can be almost as thin as paper!

Go to pages 38–39 for activities.

9 Computers

People invented the first computers more than 60 years ago. Those computers were very different from computers today.

One of the first computers was called *ENIAC*. It was built in about 1946. *ENIAC* was big and heavy. It weighed about 30 metric tons! It was also expensive – it cost about 500,000 dollars!

Over the next 40 years computers became smaller and cheaper. From about 1980 people started using computers at home. Then in 1989 Tim Berners-Lee invented the World Wide Web, or the Web.

ENIAC

Computers today are very useful. You see images on a monitor and you use a keyboard to type words. You use a mouse to move the cursor and click on buttons. To connect to the Internet you use a modem.

Modern computers also have speakers so you can listen to music or watch movies. You need a printer to print documents, and to play computer games you need a joystick. What other things can computers do?

cursor

speaker

printer

Password

****

Submit

monitor

modem

joystick

keyboard

mouse

headphones

Go to pages 40–41 for activities.

Big and Small

With modern technology, we can build machines that are very big or very small.

The cruise ship *Oasis of the Seas* is one of the world's largest passenger vehicles. It's 65 meters high and 360 meters long. It carries 5,400 passengers. It has restaurants, shops, cinemas, and three swimming pools!

The *Bagger 288* is a mining machine. It's 96 meters high and 240 meters long. It's one of the world's heaviest land vehicles. It weighs 13,500 metric tons!

The *DENSO Micro-Car* is one of the world's smallest machines. It's about 4.8 millimeters long and 1.7 millimeters high. It's smaller than a finger! The car can move, but its top speed is only 180 meters per hour. In the future people will use micro-machines like this to repair other machines from the inside.

Discover!

Scientists want to build micro-machines called nanobots. We will need a microscope to see them! Doctors will use them to help people who are sick. The nanobots will work inside their bodies.

→ Go to pages 42–43 for activities.

1 The First Machines

← Read pages 4–5.

1 Write the words. ~~stone~~ wood bone metal

1 _stone_ 3 _____

2 _____ 4 _____

2 Complete the sentences.

1 The axe is made of _stone and wood_ .
2 The knife is made of _____ .
3 The lever is made of _____ .
4 The plow is made of _____ .
5 The arrow is made of _____ .
6 The bow is made of _____ .

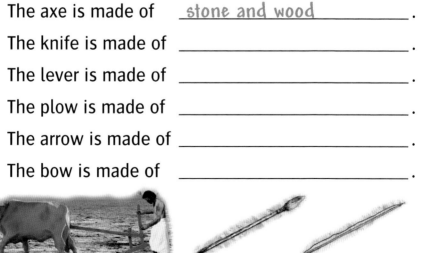

3 Complete the sentences.

tools   levers   ~~machines~~   plows   wood   farming

1 People started using _machines_ about two million years ago.

2 They used long pieces of _____ to make levers.

3 People started _____ for food about 7,000 years ago.

4 They invented farming machines like _____ .

5 Some farmers used _____ to get water.

6 People started making metal _____ about 5,000 years ago.

4 Answer the questions.

1 What did people use to shoot arrows?

People used bows to shoot arrows.

2 What did people build to get water for their plants?

_____

3 How did people move heavy objects like rocks?

_____

4 When did people start making metal tools?

_____

2 Round and Round

← Read pages 6–7.

1 Write the words.

axle   cart   clay pot
rollers   wheel   car

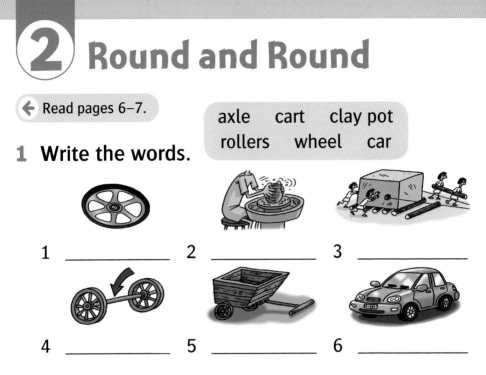

1 _____   2 _____   3 _____

4 _____   5 _____   6 _____

2 Match. Then write the sentences.

People used rollers   is a very big wheel.
An axle is a bar   to move heavy objects.
Potters used wheels   are vehicles with wheels.
The London Eye   that connects two wheels.
Carts and chariots   to make clay pots.

1 _People used rollers to move heavy objects._

2 _____

3 _____

4 _____

5 _____

3 Write *true* or *false*.

1 People used the first wheel about
2,000 years ago.   _false_

2 People made rollers from tree trunks. _____

3 Cars usually have wheels and axles.   _____

4 The first wheels were made of metal. _____

5 The London Eye is 153 meters high.   _____

4 Write the words.

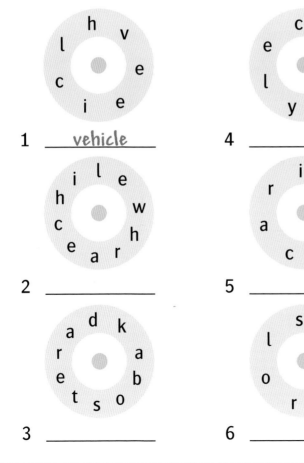

1 ___vehicle___   4 _____

2 _____   5 _____

3 _____   6 _____

3 Ramps and Cranes

← Read pages 8–9.

1 Write the words.

block   crane   pulley   ramp   rope   temple

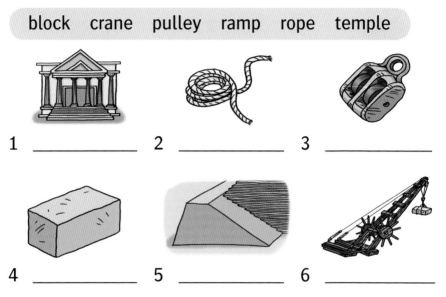

1 _____   2 _____   3 _____

4 _____   5 _____   6 _____

2 Complete the sentences.

blocks   cranes   pulleys   ramps   ropes   workers

1 The Egyptians used _____ to build pyramids.

2 The _____ of stone were very large and heavy.

3 The Egyptians needed rollers and many _____ .

4 The Greeks used big _____ made of wood.

5 The Greeks had cranes with many ropes and _____ .

6 The workers pulled the _____ and lifted the blocks.

3 Answer the questions.

1 What do ramps help us to do?

_____

2 Why did the Egyptians need many workers?

_____

3 How did the workers move the blocks up the ramps?

_____

4 Where is the biggest pyramid in Egypt?

_____

5 How high is the biggest pyramid?

_____

4 Complete the puzzle.

The Greeks (1)___ cranes to build their temples. The workers (2)___ the ropes to blocks of stone. Then they (3)___ the ropes around the pulleys. The workers (4)___ the blocks when they (5)___ the ropes. The Greeks (6)___ workers, but not as many as the Egyptians.

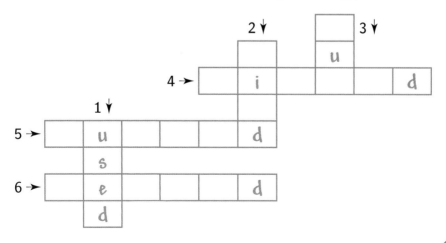

4 Water and Wind

← Read pages 10–11.

1 Write the words.

arm   axle   river   sail
millstone   watermill
wheel   windmill

1 _____

2 _____

3 _____

4 _____

5 _____

6 _____

7 _____

8 _____

2 Write *true* or *false*.

1 People use watermills to make bread. _____

2 Windmills only work when it's windy. _____

3 Watermills don't use energy from nature. _____

4 We can use windmills to produce electricity. _____

5 Watermills are useful in places with no rivers. _____

6 People used windmills thousands of years ago. _____

3 **Complete the sentences.**

> arms   axle   grain   flour
> sails   water   wheel   wind

1 Watermills can make grain into _____ .

2 Watermills use energy from flowing _____ .

3 A watermill has a large _____ on the outside.

4 The wheel turns an _____ inside the watermill.

5 Windmills use energy from the _____ .

6 A windmill has long arms with big _____ .

7 The _____ turn when the wind pushes the sails.

8 A millstone breaks the _____ .

4 **Complete the puzzle. Write the secret word.**

1 A watermill __ a wheel.   4 The millstone __ the grain.

2 A windmill __ when it's windy.   5 The wind __ a windmill's sails.

3 The wheel __ a big axle.

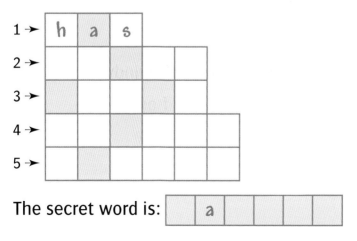

The secret word is:

5 Telling the Time

← Read pages 12–13.

1 Write the words.

digital clock   sand clock
mechanical clock   sundial
water clock

1 _____

2 _____

3 _____

4 _____

5 _____

2 Complete the chart.

batteries   gears   pots   glass bubbles   water
~~pendulum~~   pointer   sand   springs   sun

Sundial	Water Clock	Sand Clock	Mechanical Clock	Digital Clock
			pendulum	

3 Write *true* or *false*.

1 A sundial's pointer makes a shadow to tell the time. _____

2 Sand clocks had glass bubbles with water in them. _____

3 On a digital clock we can see the time in numbers. _____

4 Most cell phones and computers have clocks in them. _____

5 In water clocks the water flows from the bottom to the top. _____

6 All mechanical clocks have gears and a pendulum. _____

4 Find and write the words.

j	d	i	g	i	t	a	l
v	b	s	a	n	d	t	k
s	a	r	u	l	w	o	m
p	t	e	s	t	m	w	e
r	t	b	u	b	l	k	c
i	e	m	n	u	r	c	h
n	r	u	d	b	n	o	a
g	i	n	i	b	h	l	n
o	e	x	a	l	c	c	i
p	s	a	l	e	t	s	c
s	c	y	r	p	a	z	a
s	h	a	d	o	w	q	l

1 _digital_

2 _____

3 _____

4 _____

5 _____

6 _____

7 _____

8 _____

9 _____

10 _____

6 Engines and Energy

← Read pages 14–15.

1 Write the words.

biodiesel   boat   bus   car   coal   diesel   oil
gasoline   helicopter   plane   train   wood

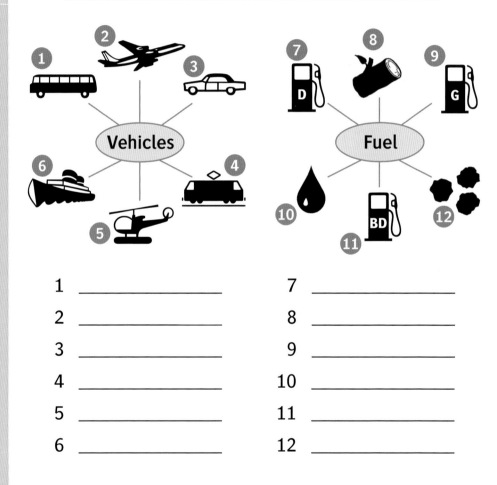

1 _____   7 _____

2 _____   8 _____

3 _____   9 _____

4 _____   10 _____

5 _____   11 _____

6 _____   12 _____

2 Order the words. Then write _true_ or _false_.

1 long / can / Buses / distances. / travel

   Buses can travel long distances.   _____

2 many / use / Today / wood. / vehicles

   _____   _____

3 cars / from / use / Electric / batteries. / energy

   _____   _____

4 and / human / Trains / energy. / use / planes

   _____   _____

5 from / made / is / materials. / Biodiesel / plant

   _____   _____

3 Answer the questions.

1 What fuels do most vehicles use today?

   _____

2 What vehicles don't produce smoke or pollution?

   _____

3 What types of vehicles use human energy?

   _____

4 What types of vehicles do you normally use?

   _____

   _____

7 Flying Machines

← Read pages 16–17.

airship   helicopter   plane
jet engine   propeller
hot-air balloon

1 Write the words.

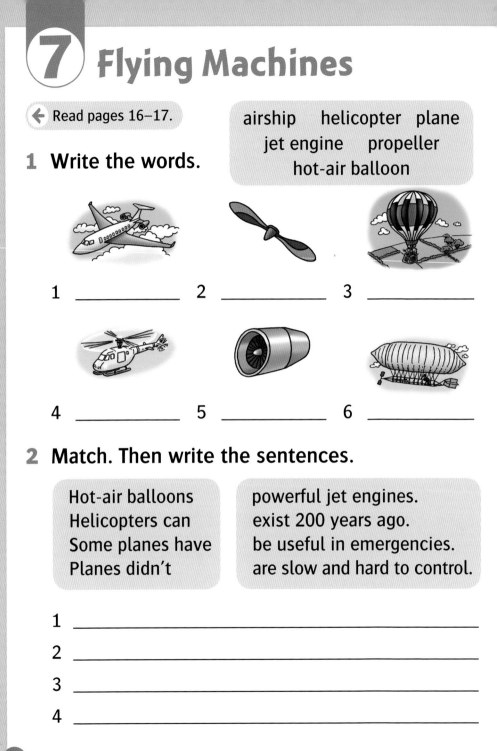

1 _____   2 _____   3 _____

4 _____   5 _____   6 _____

2 Match. Then write the sentences.

Hot-air balloons	powerful jet engines.
Helicopters can	exist 200 years ago.
Some planes have	be useful in emergencies.
Planes didn't	are slow and hard to control.

1 _____

2 _____

3 _____

4 _____

3 Write *true* or *false*.

1 Orville and Wilbur Wright invented the first jet plane. _____

2 The first plane flight in history was 12 seconds long. _____

3 Paul Comu flew one of the world's first helicopters in 1903. _____

4 Comu's helicopter floated in the air for about 20 minutes. _____

5 The world's first plane only carried one person at a time. _____

4 Complete the puzzle. Write the secret word.

1 Some types of planes only carry ___ .
2 Some planes have ___ to make them fly.
3 A hot-air balloon can fly but it doesn't have an ___ .
4 Some big planes can carry 850 ___ .
5 Helicopters can take people to ___ .
6 The *GEN H-4* ___ can carry one person.

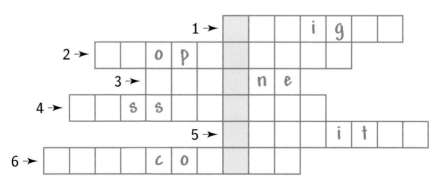

The secret word is: ⬚⬚⬚⬚⬚⬚⬚

8 Communications

← Read pages 18–19.

1 Complete the sentences.

radios   telephones   televisions   satellites   sounds
cell phones   images   messages   programs   wires

1 Old _____ transmitted _____ through wires.

2 Old _____ showed black and white _____.

3 _____ can transmit sounds with no _____.

4 Modern _____ can send text _____.

5 Now _____ transmit lots of television _____.

2 Match. Then write the sentences.

John Logie Baird	the telephone	in 1895.
Guglielmo Marconi	the first television	in 1944.
Inventors	the radio	in 1876.
Alexander Graham Bell	the color television	in 1926.

1 _____

2 _____

3 _____

4 _____

3 Find and write the words.

awavoeet(communicate)wsbphotoonowireen

messageadscreenoradioosoundgolimage

amtransmittinventnsatellitecfprogramm

communicate   _____

_____   _____

_____   _____

_____   _____

_____   _____

_____

4 Answer the questions.

1 How many televisions are there in your home?

_____

2 How many people in your family have a cell phone?

_____

3 What programs do you watch on television?

_____

4 How often do you watch movies on DVD?

_____

9 Computers

← Read pages 20–21.

1 Write the words.

cursor   joystick   keyboard
modem   monitor   mouse
printer   speaker   headphones

1 _____
2 _____
3 _____
4 _____
5 _____
6 _____
7 _____
8 _____
9 _____

2 Circle the correct words.

1 The first computers were very (big) / small and heavy.

2 The *ENIAC* computer weighed **3** / **30** metric tons.

3 The *ENIAC* computer was very **cheap** / **expensive**.

4 From **1960** / **1980** people used home computers.

5 The **Web** / **modem** was invented in 1989.

3 **Complete the sentences.**

play games   type words   use the Internet   watch movies
click on buttons   print documents   listen to music

1 You can _____ on the monitor.

2 You use a printer to _____ .

3 You need a joystick to _____ .

4 You _____ with the keyboard.

5 You use a mouse to _____ .

6 You need a modem to _____ .

7 You can _____ if you have speakers.

4 **Answer the questions.**

1 When was the *ENIAC* computer built?

_____

2 How much did the *ENIAC* computer cost?

_____

3 What did Tim Berners-Lee invent?

_____

4 What can we move with a mouse?

_____

5 What do you use a computer for?

_____

10 Big and Small

← Read pages 22–23.

1 Write the numbers.

1.7 13,500 ~~96~~ 4.8 360 180 65 240 5,400

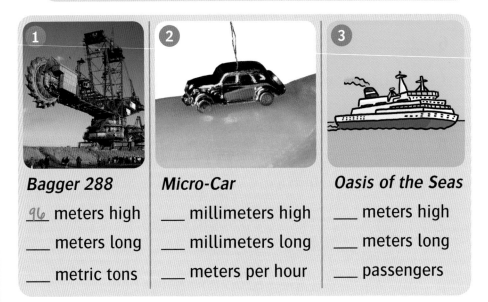

1 Bagger 288

_96_ meters high

___ meters long

___ metric tons

2 Micro-Car

___ millimeters high

___ millimeters long

___ meters per hour

3 Oasis of the Seas

___ meters high

___ meters long

___ passengers

2 Write the words.

1 r^{c}u^{s}ie $_i$hs^p _____

2 ni^{m}n^{i}g $_i$namche _____

3 r^{i}cm^{i}c^{o}s$_c$^{o}p _____

4 sar^{p}n$_s$^{e}ge _____

5 ce$_v$hi$_l$e _____

6 t^{i}s^{c}s$_i$^{e}nt$_s$ _____

3 Write *true* or *false*.

1 The *Oasis* can carry lots of people. _____

2 The *Bagger* is a large passenger vehicle. _____

3 The *Oasis* is much taller than the *Bagger*. _____

4 Doctors will use nanobots to help people. _____

5 The *Micro-Car* can move, but it's not very fast. _____

6 Nanobots are bigger than the *Micro-Car*. _____

7 The *Bagger* is heavier than the *Micro-Car*. _____

8 The *Micro-Car* is bigger than a finger. _____

4 Answer the questions.

1 What type of machine is the *Bagger*?

_____

2 What will doctors use nanobots for in the future?

_____

3 How many swimming pools does the *Oasis* have?

_____

4 What big machines do you use?

_____

_____

5 What small machines do you use?

_____

_____

A Machines Survey

1 Write two more questions for the survey.

2 Interview your friends and family. Write ✓ for each answer.

	Yes	No
1 Can you ride a bicycle?		
2 Do you usually wear a watch?		
3 Do you have a computer at home?		
4 Are there windmills near your home?		
5 Do you sometimes walk up ramps?		
6 Do you have a digital clock?		
7 Do you send text messages?		
8 Does your family's car use biodiesel?		
9 Do you sometimes travel by plane?		
10 Do you play computer games?		
11		
12		

3 Count the answers. Make a summary to show your results. Display your results.

A Machine Poster

1 Find or draw pictures of a machine that you like.

2 Answer these questions and make notes.

What does the machine do?

How does the machine work?

What can people use it for?

Who invented it? When?

3 Make a poster. Write sentences to describe the machine. Display your poster.

Picture Dictionary

 axle

 batteries

 bone

 canal

 cart

 chariot

 coal

 cord

 cruise ship

 electricity

 engine

 flour

 food

 freight

 fuel

 grain

 handle

 hot-air balloon

medicine

 metal

 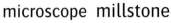  

microscope   millstone   oil   passengers   pendulum

rope   sand clock   satellite   smoke   steam

stick   stone   temple   tools   tree trunk

water clock   wheel   wheelchair   wires   wood

Oxford Read and Discover

Series Editor: Hazel Geatches • CLIL Adviser: John Clegg

Oxford Read and Discover graded readers are at four levels, from 3 to 6, suitable for students from age 8 and older. They cover many topics within three subject areas, and can support English across the curriculum, or Content and Language Integrated Learning (CLIL).

Available for each reader:
• Audio CD Pack (book & audio CD)
• Activity Book

For Teacher's Notes & CLIL Guidance go to
www.oup.com/elt/teacher/readanddiscover

Subject Area / Level	The World of Science & Technology	The Natural World	The World of Arts & Social Studies
3 600 headwords	• How We Make Products • Sound and Music • Super Structures • Your Five Senses	• Amazing Minibeasts • Animals in the Air • Life in Rainforests • Wonderful Water	• Festivals Around the World • Free Time Around the World
4 750 headwords	• All About Plants • How to Stay Healthy • Machines Then and Now • Why We Recycle	• All About Desert Life • All About Ocean Life • Animals at Night • Incredible Earth	• Animals in Art • Wonders of the Past
5 900 headwords	• Materials to Products • Medicine Then and Now • Transportation Then and Now • Wild Weather	• All About Islands • Animal Life Cycles • Exploring Our World • Great Migrations	• Homes Around the World • Our World in Art
6 1,050 headwords	• Cells and Microbes • Clothes Then and Now • Incredible Energy • Your Amazing Body	• All About Space • Caring for Our Planet • Earth Then and Now • Wonderful Ecosystems	• Helping Around the World • Food Around the World

For younger students, **Dolphin Readers** Levels Starter, 1, and 2 are available.